Being Delivered Through Hard Times

By

Guy Gray and Cheryl Ward-Kaiser

DORRANCE PUBLISHING CO
EST. 1920
PITTSBURGH, PENNSYLVANIA 15238

Dorrance Publishing Co
585 Alpha Drive
Suite 103
Pittsburgh, PA 15238
Visit our website at *www.dorrancebookstore.com*

ISBN: 979-8-88925-102-6
eISBN: 979-8-88925-602-1

Foreword

Being Delivered through Hard Times is a story of exalted faith told from the alternating perspectives of two incredible survivors. Once strangers, Cheryl Ward-Kaiser and Guy Gray came to see how perfectly their life stories complete the other. An adoptee and a mother who placed her son for adoption discover each other as the unexpected answer to their prayers, a clue into the mindset of the person they quest for, and the hope for reunification. Cheryl and Guy recount the experiences, and trauma, of their lives that simultaneously challenged and reinforced their faith more than any would think possible.

I was honored with the privilege of reading their story and soon realized their genius in two parts—first, lives as implausibly challenging as theirs have been, and the courage needed to survive them, could only act as a beacon of inspiration to others. And second, that faith tested as often as theirs has been, and as inexplicably carried through to the radical healing of everyone touched by these wonderful human beings, could only have one explanation—clearly, God has a plan for them. In their own words, Cheryl and Guy guide us by the hand through the most heart-wrenching moments of their lives, just to prove to us that their faith is what pulled them through. This story is an absolute must-read and will definitively restore the faith of all who read it and change our lives for Good.

Thank you, Guy and Cheryl, for your passion and refusal to let pain and suffering go unanswered by faith and love.

God bless you,
Nicholas Orrick

Contents

Author's Note

An adoptee and birth mother meet and talk about life's situations from each of their perspectives. Through a combined experience, they are each able to accomplish their goals when those around them thought they would fail.

Disclaimer

1. Be prepared for tough situations in this book. If you hang with this, we will get you to the other side.
2. We are not doctors or psychologists or religious leaders. We are telling our personal stories. We are not attempting to give advice.

If your life is like a small boat and the events of your life are the conditions of the water, you see the water as sometimes calm, sometimes rough, and sometimes stormy. As you approach and deal with adoption issues, it seems like you are confronted with your own private tsunami.

CHAPTER 1
How I Met Your Mother

by Guy

This chapter, written by an adoptee, is written to the son of Cheryl Ward-Kaiser, who is also an adoptee. Cheryl and I have been good friends since we met in 1990. I have met Cheryl's son a few times, but until I wrote this he did not know what led up to his mother contacting him in 1991.

About Guy.

I was placed for adoption at birth. Being adopted, I have a couple of quirky things from my childhood that are with me today. One of them has to do with failure. If you think of what a newborn's mission is after birth, it is one thing: Find your mother. This opportunity was taken from me as I was adopted in a closed adoption, but my instinct was to find my mother—and I failed. I react to failure at anything today with a PTSD-type reaction. When you see heroic things that I have done, it is less out of ego and more out of fear of failure. In my adult life, I do not fail often. When I do fail, it is a big deal.

When I was five, my grandmother told me and one of my sisters that we had been born into another family and adopted into the family that we currently lived in. She showed me that I had unique thumbs, which don't bend. She told me that this was a trait passed down to me by my mother. We were all sitting in our backyard in Vallejo under an apple tree. I asked my parents about being adopted, and they told me a few things. Yes, I was

1

adopted. They didn't know who was responsible for giving birth to me, but through a legal process I was adopted and belonged in this family now. I was told that my mother may have been an exchange student, perhaps from England. She had thumbs that didn't bend, and she may have been studying psychology. My father was believed to be Jewish. Until I was twenty-eight, this was everything I knew.

To understand my story, you need to understand a few things about the people who were in my life. I was very stubborn, rebellious, and confident. I had these qualities in gross excess. I pushed myself, and others, with a reckless abuse of reality and a pure desire to accomplish my mission.

My parents had neighbors they were very close to. The family had come to California from the Netherlands at about the time that I was born. They had three children. The father, Pieter, was in construction. He worked as an independent contractor and remodeled homes. His work was a piece of art. I remember seeing their house when I was young. I was impressed by the detail and how pretty the woodwork looked. Events in Pieter's life played a strong role in shaping my character; specifically, when he was told his outlook was hopeless, he recovered anyway.

In 1966 and then again in 1978, Pieter was involved in two very serious construction accidents. In 1966 a five-gallon bucket of glue caught on fire as someone had lit a pilot light while Pieter was carrying the glue to where he was going to put down a countertop in a kitchen. The fire severely burned his arms and face. His body and legs were also burned. When Pieter was seen by the doctor in the hospital, his wife was told not to expect him to live. Pieter spent a long time in the hospital and a long time recovering at home, but he eventually pulled through. We visited the family several times. I saw Pieter with bandages all over his arms and with burns all over his face. One time I was in a room nearby while his wife dressed his wounds as he took a bath. He yelled in Dutch very loudly for what seemed like a few minutes. I could tell he was in a lot of pain.

In 1978 he fell off a ladder and broke his back. Once again, the doctors told his wife that he would not make it. His wife visited my mother in Napa many times and gave reports on her husband's condition. Over and over, she said that he was going to die. Eventually he started to recover.

Two steel rods were placed in his back to support parts of his backbone that would not recover. He was told he would never walk again.

He spent a long time in physical therapy and eventually regained strength in his legs.

He was told that he would live a limited life. Not a month after getting out of the hospital, he walked from his home in Napa to Clearlake, about fifty-five miles. He walked by himself, nonstop. He got to his destination in fewer than two days. In spite of considerable pain, he took up golf. He moved to Clear Lake and spent much of his time golfing, even up to this day. He continued to work, and he and his wife manage a resort on Clear Lake. They are responsible for the upkeep of many trailers and homes on the property. I visited him a few years ago, when he was eighty-three. On that day, he was painting the inside of one of the houses.

In February 1980, a very good friend from high school, Dan, announced that he had congestive heart failure. Dan said that without a heart transplant, he would die. He also said that even with a heart transplant, he would likely live fewer than five years. At the time, heart transplant surgery was considered experimental. Doctors were able to perform transplants, but the body would reject the new organ and the medication that was available at the time was not good enough to promote long-term life. Patients were told that with a successful surgery, one might live five additional years.

Dan was told that he was going to die very shortly after Pieter had walked to Clear Lake. With Pieter's story in mind, Pieter's wife and I told Dan, rather sternly, not to believe the doctors if the doctors said he was going to die.

I always thought it was God's doing putting Pieter's story right in front of Dan's situation at that time.

The process for getting the transplant was long and tedious. The family had to go under a psychological evaluation, as they needed to make sure that everyone could handle the emotional and physical challenges that Dan would have while waiting for a transplant and beyond. They had to raise money. There were fundraising drives at school, and he was in the paper and on the news. Everyone in town knew who Dan was, and everyone was rooting for him. One of the people who called and talked to Dan was the mother of Dick Vermeil, head coach of the Philadelphia Eagles. The Eagles made it to the Super Bowl that year, and Dick's mother and Dan talked about football.

Bob Knepper, the pitcher for the Giants, also visited Dan. He gave Dan a Sony Walkman so that Dan could listen to music while being kept awake at night because of his condition.

He had a letter from singer Amy Grant as well. She had a song, "My Father's Eyes," that Dan was partial to.

Dan was given a ten-speed bike by a sixth-grade girl who won it in a raffle. She told Dan that he would need a bike when he recovered.

Dan's story brought the best out of people in Napa and beyond. At the same time, the support of a loving public greatly encouraged Dan when he decided to fight his physical condition instead of giving up.

Additionally, there was the waiting. Dan and several others were waiting for someone to die so that they could receive a heart.

During 1980 Dan had several heart attacks and nearly died three times. Each of these times, his last rites had been given to him by the priest. His father called me after the third time, Thanksgiving weekend, and told me that he wasn't going to make it. At the time, I was a first-year student at UC Davis, majoring in Mathematics. This was a trying time for me as schoolwork was hard. I decided that my support of my friend's condition was a priority. From this point forward, I spent my weekends in Palo Alto at Stanford Medical Center, visiting Dan and his family. Dan had indicated to me that his medical journey was a journey of faith. It was Dan's belief that God wanted him to get a transplant and survive. Dan's goal was to promote a Christian ministry based on his healing testimony.

Each week when I visited Dan, we talked about something that was concerning him, often very deeply. One weekend he told me, "I have the best doctors in the world, and they tell me that I am going to die. What am I doing here? Why am I continuing to fight when I am going to die anyway?"

I reminded Dan that his journey was one of faith. I asked him, "Which has more power in your life? Is it the opinion of the best doctors in the world, or is it the degree of your faith?"

He told me that it was his faith. I told him to live the rest of his life, every breath, only in that faith.

And he did.

On December 22, 1980, he received a heart transplant and ended up living until 2009, a long time after the original five years that had been given to him by the doctors in the event he had his transplant surgery. Dan fought physical rejection during his transplant and recovery. His body basically tried to kill the foreign heart that the doctors had put in him. It was important for me later to understand the role of rejection when my birth mother was not willing to accept my contact several years later.

I got married in 1983 to my high school sweetheart. Dan was my best man. By 1987 my wife and I had two children. In October of that year, I was offered a computer job working for a Fresh Western, a produce marketing company in Salinas. I uprooted my young family, and we moved to Salinas.

In 1988 living in Salinas, my wife and I were saving every penny that we had so we could purchase our first home. We found a new subdivision in Pine Canyon in King City. The new homes were inexpensive and were the only things that we could possibly afford, but they were still out of our price range as I had a lot of debt from college.

In October, the Oakland A's, my favorite team, had made it to the World Series. I told about five friends in my office, "I am going to the World Series!" They all laughed. One reminded me that the tickets, if I could find any, would cost several hundred dollars. I told them all, very sure of myself, that I was going. My friend Dennis questioned my common sense and grip on reality. I told him that when I focus on something, I get what I want. I spent all afternoon bragging about going to the World Series, when in reality I had no hope.

After being teased for the last time and tired of their lack of faith in me, I walked into the next office and talked to the president of our company. I had never been there before, and I was not sure that he would know who I was. I told him, "I do not have any money, and I would really love to go to the World Series and watch the Oakland A's play. If someone gives you free tickets, would you consider giving them to me?" He didn't say a word, and then I walked out.

The next day, he called me into his office and gave me two tickets to the World Series with VIP parking.

This was Game 3, in Oakland, against the Los Angeles Dodgers. It was the only game of the series that Oakland won.

The next year, San Francisco and Oakland both made it to the World Series. During the day of Game 3, I had been building emergency communication equipment for our computer system. If the communication system died, we would still be able to communicate to our remote sites.

Just before 5 P.M., I got a call from the title company. My wife and I were to go down the following day and sign papers so that we could purchase our first home. After the phone call, I rolled the cart, which contained the equipment, into a vault in my office. As I let go of the rack, the Loma Prieta earthquake hit. I could hear the earthquake for at least three seconds before I felt it. It sounded like an eighteen-wheel truck driving through our building. I thought I was going to die. When I did feel the earthquake, the ground was going up and down, and it was hard to stand up in one spot. I quickly ran to get under my desk, which was in the next room.

Stress from buying a house, dealing with work problems related to the earthquake, and not knowing if my family members were okay became too much for me. For the first time, I felt a need to know if my birth mother was okay, and I needed to contact her. Before that, I was never really that interested in finding her.

In December, I contacted Social Services in Vallejo. They provided me with a letter with non-identifying information about my birth mother. Late in January, I had my mother contact her lawyer from the 1960s, and she was able to get my birth mother's name. A letter from Social Services confirmed that my mother's thumbs did not bend, but it also said that she had a brother with the same thumbs. It was of interest because I later found out that C. S. Lewis also had thumbs that did not bend. Also, she was Jewish, not my father.

I mailed eight letters to people with my birth mother's last name, asking for genetic information about people that had thumbs that didn't bend. A few days later, I was in touch with an adoption support group, called Search Finders, out of San Jose. A woman named Dot[1] gave me the name, address, and phone number of my birth mother. She lived in San Francisco.

Once I had my birth mother's address and phone number, I acted on impulse. I picked up the phone and called her—no answer but I heard her voice on the answering machine. So cool. I called back just to hear her voice. I did this over and over again because her voice was so fascinating. She never answered the phone.

I was so excited; I was beside myself. Common sense had left me. On Valentine's Day, I left home at three o'clock in the morning with a letter about myself. I got to her house sometime after six. I just waited and watched as her neighbors began their day. About 8:30 A.M., I knocked on her door. No answer. Over the next thirty minutes or so, I knocked a few more times and then gave up.

I left the letter for her. In addition to identifying who I was, I left her contact information for Search Finders as well as contact information from Social Services. I drove home and went to work. I was still so excited.

The next day, just before lunch, I got a call from Social Services. "The woman that you contacted has requested in no uncertain terms that you are to never contact her again." The woman on the other end of the line told me that she had never talked to anyone who was this upset. She was absolutely hysterical and had a hard time getting her message across. She said that if I contacted her again, she would contact a lawyer.

I was not prepared for this. I didn't know how to fail.

My friend Dennis' father, who was a lawyer, was a prominent member of his church. I asked Dennis if he could put me in touch with his father, and within an hour I was in his office.

Dennis Sr. welcomed me in, and I told him my story. He was deeply concerned. He asked if we could pray about my situation—and I was glad to do so. He told me that a woman at his church had given a speech about "consequences for your actions." The message was to young people. She was telling them not to have sex so that they would not repeat the mistake that she had made. She had also told people that she was a birth mother. He suggested that maybe I should talk to her. Her name was Cheryl Ward.

Cheryl was a volunteer at a crisis pregnancy center in Salinas, and that is where we met. I had never been to a place like this, but I can assure you, when I walked in I was more upset than anyone else in the building. This meeting provided the first time that I had ever talked to a birth mother and the first time that she had ever talked to an adoptee. We were both fascinated with each other's story, and when we finished sharing she asked me what I hoped to gain from all this.

I told her that if we could be in a room together and for it to no longer be a problem for either of us, that is what I would hope to gain.

She told me, "I gave a son up for adoption. I will never contact him. I hurt him once…what right do I have to hurt him again? But if he ever got married, I would love to be invited to his wedding."

These messages were important to each of us. Each time we talked, we reminded each other of the thing we wanted most. It was something we spelled out during our first meeting.

About a month later, I went to see Cheryl again at the crisis pregnancy center. I had mailed those letters about the thumbs—eight letters—and I had received responses from five, all the wrong family. Then I got a random phone call: "Who are you, and what do you want?" She wanted to know how I found the family and if I were a doctor. I was not ready for contact, so I made something up and then went on my way.

Cheryl and I talked about how cool this was. I told her that this was my aunt, my uncle's wife. I didn't know what to do, so I gave myself some time to think about it.

In July, four months later, I called my aunt back. "My name is Guy. I have reason to believe that I am your husband's nephew." She told me that there was no way, that I was making this up. I told her my thumbs did not bend and neither did my children's.

She told me, "Your thumbs bend. So do mine." I informed her that they did not.

Long pause. "Oh. Send me some pictures." So, I did.

A few days later, I was having dinner with my aunt, uncle, two cousins, and the husband of one cousin.

Cheryl and I met again to talk about my progress. It was still a very painful matter that I could not resolve anything with my mother, but things were happening for me.

A short time later, my aunt and uncle visited us in our new home in King City. I also met another cousin and my half-brother.

Nobody had known about me. I was a big secret. In November, I met a half-sister, and by this time I had met everyone except my mom and one half-sister.

In the spring, Cheryl and I talked again. I assured her that even though things were moving for me, I was not finished. I also told her, "I think that you should search for your son."

Immediately, she said no and told me all of her reasons again. I listened.

Then I told her, "I think you should meet your son. You can find him; I can help."

She insisted, "No, I can't do that."

I said, "Even though I am not your son, I give you permission to look for him."

A week later, she called me. "Tell me again what I need to do to get started…."

CHAPTER 2
Meeting Brett and the Crime

by Cheryl

After Guy gave me permission to find my son, I decided I was ready.

I went to Search Finders in San Jose, California, and they called me back in eighteen days with my son's name: Brett Alan Paton—6 feet, 2 inches tall, 210 pounds, brown hair, brown eyes.

I called Dot, the woman from Search Finders, and said, "How do I do this?"

She said, "Write down all your questions," so I did.

I called him, and his roommate answered the phone. I asked for Brett.

"Wait a minute. I'll get him."

My son—my twenty-six-year-old son—was coming to the phone. I was shaking so badly and had never been so nervous.

When he came to the phone, I said what the people from Search Finders suggested I say: "Hello, Brett, this is a very private and personal conversation. Do you have a few minutes?"

He said, "I'm on my way out of the door."

I was thinking, *Too bad ,guy! We are a go. I can't do this tomorrow.*

"Is your name Brett Alan Paton?"

"Yep, that is my name!"

"Were you born on June 6, 1964?"

"Yep, that is when I was born."

Wouldn't you think he would have thought about this phone call happening? But he had no idea what I was going to say.

The next question was the toughest for us birthparents; we don't want to be the one who tells them they are adopted. I had gotten non-identifying information about him three weeks before I found him. It said that his parents were going to be very open with him about his adoption. I knew that he knew he was adopted.

"And you're adopted, right?" I asked.

"Yep, I'm adopted."

HE HAD NO IDEA WHAT I WAS GETTING READY TO TELL HIM.

"I'm your birth mother!"

"WOW!"

I said, "I never even knew your name until two days ago."

"WOW!" Again, it was all he could say.

I was thinking, *You are mine, but I am a motor mouth and all you can say is WOW!*

After a pause, I said, "You didn't hang up on me."

He said, "Hang up on you? I would never hang up on you!"

So open…so accepting….

He was late for class; he was going to college at the time. We talked for fifteen more minutes, and he accepted every detail I told him. He never questioned anything I had to say.

I went to meet him two months later. I had no idea what he looked like as I waited in the lobby of a Marriott hotel.

He was late. That should have told me a lot.

I was standing up and straining to watch for anyone that looked like a twenty-six-year-old young man. I saw a guy walk out in front of the glass. He looked like me. My two daughters don't even look like me. As he walked into the lobby of the hotel, I found myself looking at *my* nose, *my* baggy eyelids, *my* bags under my eyes…. *How sad, he has all my bags*, I thought. I looked at his mouth, his dimples, the big cleft in his chin, the enormous neck…. For twenty-six years I thought I knew who the father was, but no, this young man was my husband's child.

I was on tilt as he hugged me. I felt like I was in *The Wizard of Oz*, and I was melting. *Oh my God…this is my husband's child.*

Still reeling, we made our way to his truck and went to lunch in Laguna Beach. Instead of getting to ask him what kind of ice cream he liked, I had to tell him that the guy I wrote down on his birth certificate is not his father. There was this other guy that was his dad—my husband. I felt like a real slut! I was crying so bad that the waiter wouldn't even wait on us during our five-and-a-half-hour lunch.

I asked him if he would like to meet his father and his two sisters, and he said he would. We went back to the hotel to say goodbye and promised to see each other in two weeks.

I called my husband, who was at work in Yuma, Arizona. Produce workers spend half their lives in Yuma. I said, "I'm twenty-six years late, but you have a son."

His first line was "WOW." (Must be in the genes.) His second line was "Are you sure he is mine?" I told him.

I called him in Yuma two days later.

"Well…," he said, "yep, he is mine."

We came back in two weeks to meet our son, but he didn't show up. It must be a little overwhelming finding your birth mother and then discovering your birth mother and father are married and you have two full-blood sisters. In addition, his mom was not a happy camper that I found him.

Well, the ball was in his court, so we went home to wait.

Three weeks later, I got a short note: "Can we just slow this all down?"

Of course, I would not put pressure on him. It was February when we were supposed to meet, and his birthday was coming up in June. I wanted to send him a card for his birthday but try picking out that card! I wanted my husband to sign the card as well. Now, he hated to write and didn't really send cards. I don't know if you are aware of this, but we girls are really good at pushing men's buttons, and when you are married you are even better at it. I walked up to my husband thinking I was going to tell him what to write, and I heard a very loud voice inside of me say, *Shut up, Cheryl.* The miracle of miracles is that I kept quiet and handed him the card. He wrote: "Son, I would like to meet you someday. Love, Jamie." He called him son but didn't sign it "Dad."

Eight days later, my husband Jamie, Roxie (my seventeen-year-old daughter), and I were home in bed. I heard a noise in the other part of the house and thought Roxie had gotten up and gotten sick. Then I heard another noise in the hallway.

I got up on my elbow and looked at the clock: 2:13 in the morning.

Then two very large men burst into our bedroom with a handgun and a shotgun. The one with the shotgun racked that shotgun so we would know it was loaded. We never even got out of bed.

The one with the handgun came to my husband's side of the bed, and the one with the shotgun came to my side of the bed. He pointed the shotgun in my face. They pulled my husband out of bed and put him face up with the handgun in his mouth. He beat the hell out of Jamie with the barrel of the handgun. The guy with the shotgun pulled me across the bed and put me face down with my hands up.

Then there were four of them. Two stayed with us, and two went to get my seventeen-year-old daughter. I cannot describe to you what it feels like to know that you cannot stop what is happening to your family. They talked forever to bring her into our bedroom. Then they threw her on the floor and kicked her. They picked me up and hit me with the shotgun.

These guys had been told that we had a safe with money in it. We *do not* have a safe, and there is no money. My husband is a cooler manager; we don't own anything. We don't have any reason to have a safe. But they believed it with everything they had.

They made my daughter stand on our bed and strip off her clothes. He put the shotgun in her mouth and said he was going to blow her f__'n head off. I knew what that would look like. It is amazing what your mind's eye can do.

Not enough. He raped her with the barrel of that shotgun. Still not enough. He turned to my husband and said, "We are going to rape your wife and your daughter, and we are going to make you watch."

Now, my husband had already had to watch them put the gun in her mouth and watched him rape her with the shotgun. You know, there is only so much a man, and a father, can take, and he couldn't take any more.

He stood up for the first time in forty-eight minutes. The guy with the shotgun came up behind him and hit him in the head. The shotgun went off, my husband pushed him into the bathroom, and the struggle continued into my closet. I heard a muffled shot, and then I heard a thud hit the floor.

I was lying on the bedroom floor with a man's foot on my back and a handgun to my head. Every time I talked or moved, he pushed on my back with his foot and with the gun. I didn't pick up my head when I heard that muffled shot, but I knew it was him!

The handgun guy came out of the closet like it was no big deal. "Get ahold of that f__'n bitch," he said. They were still bent on raping Roxie and still asking about the safe. Forty-eight minutes and they still believed there was a safe. I cannot tell you how many times we said there was no safe!

The lookout came running back into the room and said, "There is a car on the road, and it stopped."

With that, they left and told me not to move for fifteen minutes. Right! The moment they hit the hallway, I jumped up and headed for my closet. I had to find out if Jamie was alive or dead.

It was the longest run of my life. His eyes were open. "I'm sorry.... I'd like to stay right here." I started trying to feel for a heartbeat, but my pulse was beating so loud it was all I could hear. I screamed at Roxie to get dressed and do CPR on her dad. Guess who doesn't know CPR? She did CPR on her dad, and he breathed three breaths, then died in Roxie's arms, the most appropriate place for him to die. He died trying to save his daughter.

Eight minutes later, the sheriff's office was there. Twenty-seven hours later, we had all five of them in jail. It was very hard for me that they were teenagers: an eighteen- and nineteen-year-old, two twenty-year-old boys, and a sixteen-year-old girl who drove the getaway car. I have worked with teenagers my whole life, and the very thing I loved had invaded our home. We didn't know any of them.

The hardest thing I had to do that day was call the son I had just found and tell him his birth father was dead. He didn't come to the funeral, but he flew in a couple of months later and met his sisters.

If you don't remember anything else, please remember that I don't hate the people who did this to me. I hate what they did, but I don't hate them. But I still had to put them away and make sure they didn't hurt anyone else.

The morning after the crime, the sheriffs had every door open to my house. I was freezing…just like I am as I write this. It is so easy to feel just like it was that morning.

CHAPTER 3

Restorative Justice

by Cheryl

Years after meeting my son, I felt I needed to go see the guy I had thought was the father. I knew he was married and had a son of his own, but I just felt I owed him the truth.

How do you tell someone this and not have them panic in the telling? I went to his store, and he was the only one there. I asked him if we could go have coffee or something. He said, "I'm the only one here right now." *Oh , God…here we go!* The first thing I was saying was "I found my son, and he's not yours!" I told him about Jamie and him, about our meeting in Mission Viejo. I told him about how I could take a picture of me from the nose up and Jamie from the nose down and it would be my son. I wanted him to know the truth. All he offered was a quote: "Better to have loved and lost than not to have loved at all." How gracious.

Back in the 1960s, if you got pregnant the guy was expected to marry you. Single mom—there was no such term. I knew no one who had a child and was not married.

He didn't marry me, thank God. It wasn't his kid.

When I came back from placing my son for adoption, I felt like scum, so low I could fit under a door. I had to fight to ever think anything of myself. My parents called me lots of names, and now I had made all those names come true. The biggest word my father called me was stupid. I had become that word. I still to this day fight the feeling that I am stupid. I use the word on myself all the time. I'm seventy-seven years old, and these words stay in your head. Abuse…crisis pregnancy…I was so grateful that Jamie would even date me again.

I have been told that after high school, you were to get out or pay to live there. I have worked since I was twelve years old. I walked about a mile and a half and got in the back of an open pickup to drive to Chualar, ten miles away, to pull the weeds out of the beans of a nearby farm. The next year, I worked housekeeping at a motel. I worked with my Portuguese grandmother, Nana (everyone called her Nana). She was a pistol. She was four feet, ten inches, but she could work rings around me. That was a hot place to work.

Is it any wonder that I got pregnant? It was a way out!

I got pregnant in September, and my sister was getting married on January 4, 1964. I stayed until the wedding, and I left the next day. My car broke down about forty-five minutes out of town. I tried to get it fixed, but it broke down again. I would not call my dad or mom. I called Jamie and asked if he would come get my stuff and drive it down to Long Beach. He came with his cousin, Peggy, and we loaded up my stuff. I drove my friend Adreon's car, and he drove my stuff down. It rained the whole way. We arrived about eight o'clock in the morning. We had breakfast, and he left us in a motel.

Adreon started work, and I found an apartment and a job for me too. I found a doctor, and she recommended an adoption agency, Holy Family Adoption Agency. It was all so hard. You didn't get to pick families or get pictures…write letters…none of that! It was all so awful. The doctor was terrific, though. She really wanted to make it easy for me.

The people at the apartment didn't know I was going to place my child for adoption, so they gave me a surprise shower. I had a bassinet in my bedroom with clothes in it for weeks. I couldn't even look at them. I told everyone that the baby died. It was okay to cry…and I cried all the time.

After I first talked in Gonzales about my pregnancy, other teachers started asking me to talk as well. I talked at church youth groups, churches, and any place they asked me to talk. It made everything better. It helped in my healing about my son and about the murder. People would always say, "I thought my life was bad." It seemed to make a difference with lots of people. I wouldn't just talk about the murder; I also talked about the childhood abuse and about placing my son for adoption. Most importantly, I talked about forgiveness!

When Guy came into the crisis pregnancy center, he was looking for answers.

I told him that we, the birth parents, did what we did out of fear. Women today don't place their kids for adoption as often, so adoptees think we just threw them away, that we didn't want them. That was not true. We had a hard time explaining why we had to use adoption and how our families reacted if we weren't getting married. It would have been easier to tell my parents that I killed someone than to tell them I was pregnant. It would be seen as a reflection of their bad parenting. Somehow it was the worst thing that could happen to a family.

It was good to listen to Guy talk about being an adoptee and how he grew up. To hear how his mom reacted to him at her front door. To try to help him understand her reaction. To connect with someone in the worst-case scenario of an adoption triangle. Yet he was not deterred. I had never met anyone so determined to find his mother and father. It gave me hope.

In 1981 I had a friend who I found out was abusing her daughter. I got a call from someone at the high school I worked at asking me to come and talk to him. He asked me if it was possible that this so-called friend was capable of beating her teenage daughter. I had befriended her because she wanted to know about the Catholic Church. My answer was "Yes."

The daughter, Amy, had talked to this person at school, who called me. I talked to Amy, and she told me her horror story. How her mother would be talking to me on the phone while she had her foot on Amy's throat. How her mom gave her a perm because she had pulled out so much of her hair. I was sickened. The next thing I knew, the police called me because Amy had run away from home. They asked if I would take her in, and I did. She was a year older than Trena. My husband, Jamie, was the girl's boss.

Amy's mother started doing things to hurt my family. She called the high school and tried to get my daughter changed to another school. Thank God, the person who answered the phone felt something was wrong and called me. She also tried to get my husband fired. Then she really scared me that she wanted me to meet her in church at the altar. Her voice is…evil!

I had a group of people that I knew, and they called unexpectedly and asked me if they could pray with me. I said yes.

They prayed, and I had a born-again experience.

I describe it as a turning-on of the light. I was going to church every day, but had I really turned my life over to God and let Him take control? No, I hadn't! I needed Him to protect me. Literally.

The morning after they prayed, I loaded up all three kids—my two girls and Amy—and drove to Carmel. Before we left, Trena went back in the house and brought out something all wrapped up. It was a two-foot crucifix! We all laughed. We needed the crucifix, and we needed to laugh.

I took them all out of school. I wasn't sure what she was capable of doing to us, so we were gone by 7 A.M. We had breakfast in Carmel and drove around and didn't come home until late. I kept Amy for six weeks, and she went to counseling.

She eventually returned home. I was always scared for her, but I believed that the Lord was going to take care of her. The only thing I could do was not be her mother's friend again. That was the only real statement I could make. My life has never been the same again. Good did come from such a tragedy because the Lord became alive to me, not something out there—He was right there!

The morning that my husband was killed, I looked up and there was Amy's mother coming up my brick walkway. Someone said, "I'll talk to her," but I stopped them. "No, I'll talk to her."

I walked out and said, "Sorry, I really don't need you here." All I asked was "Does your daughter know?" She said yes and left. I still communicate with Amy all these years later.

That morning I was freezing. All I wanted to do was make some coffee. I needed a cup of something warm. Of course, they were taking fingerprints and getting evidence. Roxie and I were put in the step-down living room since we told the police they hadn't gone into that room.

Roxie looked at me and said, "My dad will never walk me down the aisle."

Six months earlier, Trena had gotten married. It was a beautiful wedding. The theme was *The Phantom of the Opera*, and I wore black. Jamie had all five of the Packard automobiles at the venue. He had worked so hard to have them all up and running. We had a procession of them from our house in the country to the church. So much for getting our hair done! They were all convertibles, and Jamie just had to have the tops down. It was magical.

Roxie's first thought was that she would never have that moment.

I looked up and saw what can only be described as a "cowboy cop" walking through the open front door. He had on cowboy boots and a black leather jacket, and his hair was swirled in a unique hairdo. All I could think was *Of course, I get a cowboy sheriff!* He brought Roxie to the den and talked to her while another sheriff interviewed me. This sheriff had booze on his breath; I found out later that he was struggling with cancer. They had not interviewed us for five minutes when they went outside for a cigarette. I thought, *They can't wait more than five minutes without a cigarette.* Unknown to me, they were discussing if I had killed my husband.

We were not crying, and we were not reacting the way they thought we should act. They came back in, and the sheriff asked me if I was okay.

I said, "I guess so."

He said, "You have insurance, right?"

I said, "Yes, I think I have $60,000 worth of insurance with the T&A Company." I had $10,000 otherwise, just enough to bury him. I had no idea that they thought I had done this. It was days before they believed that I didn't do it. Thank God for being naïve at the time and having no idea what they were thinking.

Early that morning, all the sheriffs in and around the house were all mad at something. I swear I could see steam coming out of some of their ears. I found out later that the sheriff in charge of the case and the one responsible for catching all these "twits," Investigative Sergeant Terry Kaiser, was pissing off all these guys because they weren't doing things that he needed done to catch them. Terry was yelling at them and getting them moving. In twenty-seven sleepless hours, they had them all in jail. Sergeant Kaiser had a phone in each ear and was putting sheriffs in taxi cabs, orchestrating how to take the criminals down with no casualties.

Roxie and I said, "They will never catch them." We knew we didn't know them. I cannot tell you loud enough what a difference it has made in my life that Sergeant Terry caught them. I would have spent the rest of my life looking for them. My life would have been so different.

I sat there thinking. I had no mortgage insurance, barely enough money to bury my husband, no will…. I was in trouble! I had a high school diploma and hadn't worked in twenty-six years. Now what? I called my husband's boss, Rick Antle, and his wife, Karen, answered the phone. I told Karen what had happened, and they came to my house that morning. As I talked, she said, "Sounds like the same people that robbed my family two months ago." I did not know that they had been robbed. Sure enough, they were some of the same people.

When Rick left my house that morning, he stood at the door and said, "Don't worry, Cheryl. I'll take care of you."

I walked back into my den and said to myself, "What does that mean?"

Then I heard a small voice say, *"Do you trust me?"*

It was the Lord. I knew it. And my answer was "Yes, I trust you."

With all of these guys now in jail, Deputy District Attorney Gary Meyer came to my house to talk to me about the case. Now, I know how rare that is for a DA to come to your house. I was treated differently because it was a big deal and because my husband worked for a big produce company. Jamie was a cooler manager; he wasn't an executive or a bigshot. He was a hard worker. I have always said, "If the guys in this crime had wanted a job, he would have given them a job." Not what they wanted! Little did I know how close my DAs would become to me in my life.

Because they decided to seek the death penalty, they got a second DA on my case, Albert Maldonado. Mind you, I don't believe in the death penalty. They had a meeting that they didn't let me into as they tried to figure out if they could keep my mouth shut on how I felt about the death penalty. Chuck Bardin, the cowboy sheriff, assured them he could control me. That would not be easy!

When you go through something like this, you rely on total strangers in the most difficult time in your life. These people, once strangers, became family. They were with me during the most vulnerable time in my life. I had to trust so many people with my future. All control was gone.

Sheriff Bardin told me to do something at the preliminary hearing; he told me, "Look at them." He said he wasn't going to tell me why. "Just look at them."

The courthouse people had me in the judge's chambers in the back. When I was told to come out, I took my seat on the stand. I had my hand in the pocket of my blue and white blouse wrapped around my rosary, which was holding the hand of the Blessed Mother. I looked at them as Gary, the DA, asked me the one question I had asked him to ask me: "Do you have a safe?"

They were so determined that I had a safe! They asked us over and over, "Where is the safe?" for forty-eight minutes.

As I answered Gary's question, I looked at each of the four guys sitting at the defense table, and they all looked down. They couldn't look me in the eyes or even take their eyes off the floor.

I took back my power at that moment. That is what they take from you in that room—your power. I now had power over them. I have power over them for the rest of their lives.

I also realized that I didn't hate them.

I had asked God for the desire not to hate them. I was granted that grace at that moment. I wanted to shout it out loud, but I knew Gary Meyer would have had a fit. I could breathe! I didn't hate them. What a grace granted to me.

Now, don't get me wrong; I had to put them away. They had to pay a consequence for their crime. Forgiveness is not being soft on crime; it is about freeing me from their control. They still have to be put away.

The first person we put away was the sixteen-year-old girl who drove the getaway car. We certified her as an adult. She got scared and pleaded guilty. She got fifteen years to life, but she got to serve her time in the California Youth Authority. She got off easy, as far as I was concerned. She was the girlfriend of the shooter. He would page her, and they would set up the robbery—no cell phones back then. This was June 14, 1991, but it seems like yesterday.

The next one was the one that had his foot on my back. I was held out of court the entire twenty-two months we were in court putting these guys away. I was allowed in because they were trying to take the trial to another county. While we were doing this, the guy who'd had his foot on my back stood up (no one knew he was going to do this) and said, "I am guilty, Your Honor." Then he turned around and said to me, "I am sorry what I did to you and your family." He got twenty-nine years to life.

Next was the lookout. He did a slow plea and got twenty-five years to life.

Next was the shooter, then the one who raped Roxie. The shooter was first. We brought the guy back who had his foot on my back to testify against him. I got to go downstairs in the Monterey Courthouse and sit on the bench with the guy who had his foot on my back and the gun to my head. I tried to talk him into testifying. He refused! I left crying.

His mother was in the breakroom of the courthouse, and she had her new baby with her. I took care of her baby while she talked to her son. Of course.

He testified! I told him later, "If you keep your nose clean in prison, I will get you out!" He put on a snitch's jacket for me. It put him at risk in prison. I asked the media not to print his name or put his picture on TV. One TV station put it on anyway. They paid a consequence for their actions, though. When the trial was over, I refused to give them an interview. Their quote on TV: "The victim refuses to talk to us." I gave the station that did it right an exclusive two-night interview from my bedroom. Everyone pays a consequence.

The shooter got life in prison without chance of parole—LWOP, as they call it.

Now we bring up the one who raped Roxie. The judge kept coming back and telling us he did not want to give him LWOP. I had several other judges try to talk me into a lesser charge. I was firm: He escalated the crime. His determination to rape Roxie pushed the crime and caused my husband's death. I said no. He got a guilty verdict.

The penalty phase of the trial was next. I delivered a Victim Impact Statement. I had never even served on a jury or been in court for anything. It was all new to me! But I delivered the speech of my life. I knew not to have my speech written down with me at the stand. I deliver speeches all the time to kids. I wrote it down, and I memorized it. I did not sit on the stand. I stood at the DA table, and I stood next to the guy who raped Roxie. I walked him back through his rape, and I talked like he talked and used the F word. The court had to understand what we had to listen to in our bedroom. Then I asked the judge, if it was his wife and she was standing there, what would he want her to say if their daughter had been raped and he had been murdered? I delivered a twenty-two-minute speech, and when I was finished the judge walked off the bench. He was supposed to sentence him that day, but he came back four days later with life in prison without parole. That's not vengeance; it's justice. There's a difference between the two.

I wanted to thank the person who made it possible for me to do the Victim Impact Statement. They told me his name was James Rowland; he was the Head of Corrections and the Head of the California Youth Authority. I was shocked! Why would he write the law giving us victims a voice in the courtroom? I went over to Fresno, and he was in my audience as I talked. They told me he was there, and I told that audience what giving me that voice in the courtroom meant to me. Finally, someone was going to listen to what I wanted to say.

I was able to talk with James. I wanted to know why he would write such a law. I didn't get an immediate answer.

He walked me to my car and said, "I want you to come to Fresno for a conference, and I'll pay your way and for your stay. Just trust me and come."

I went to the conference on restorative justice. He told me nothing about it beforehand, but when I left the conference I said, "This is what I fought to do. This is what I made happen. I now have a name for what I fought to do: restorative justice."

Now, it's one thing to write that I don't hate them, but I needed to tell them that I don't hate them…that I forgive them. The first one was the girl. She was going to get out first. She was sixteen when she did the crime, and they could only keep her until her twenty-fifth birthday in the California Youth Authority.

CHAPTER 4
Contacting the Prisoners

by Cheryl

In 1998, seven years later, I realized that the girl who took part in the crime would get out when she was twenty-five years old. She would have been twenty-three at the time.

I decided to write to the people who took part in the crime. After all, they owed me. Not the system…ME! I wrote to the girl and all four guys. I can remember parking next to a park and writing the guy who raped Roxie. He was the hardest to write to. Wouldn't you think it would have been the shooter? No, the rapist. How do you start such a letter? "Guess who"? I kind of started that way. I said, "I bet you never thought you would get a letter from me." I told him that I wanted to know how they were doing and what they were doing to better themselves. They all wrote me back.

I wanted to do a victim/offender mediation, but I needed to have them agree to meet with me. I needed to make friends with them. I didn't need to be a threat. They were all shocked that I would write to them. I still have all their hundreds of letters. I've never thrown one away.

In 2001 I was diagnosed with hairy cell leukemia. It is very rare; only six hundred people in the U.S. are diagnosed a year, and four out of five are men. Only sixty-five women a year are diagnosed with this cancer. It is treatable, but it took six months to diagnose. I had a liver biopsy and a bone marrow biopsy on two consecutive days. The orderly asked me if I got them "cheaper by the dozen." He made me laugh. Bone marrow is easier; the liver one hurt bad. Then the blood doctor walked by and said, "I think I know what this is… . I have a special blood test for you."

They had to send it off to Seattle. It was hairy cell leukemia. I did an infusion for seven days for my chemotherapy. Three months later, I was diagnosed with breast cancer, and in four months I had my third cancer, basal cell skin cancer—three cancers in seven months.

You know what I said? "I've been through worse. I survived a home robbery in which my husband was murdered, and my daughter raped. I can survive this!"

I went to UCSF for my breast cancer. I took a drug that shrank my cancer in half; I had a six-centimeter cancer, and we waited six months. The doctor did a lumpectomy instead of a mastectomy. I did chemo and seven weeks of radiation, and on the last day of my chemo I broke out with shingles. Shingles was, by far, worse than all my cancers. They couldn't get me to quit breaking out. Finally, they did an infusion for seven days and it quit, but of course you have all the other stages: shooting pain, itching.... I had to keep it wet, so I had large towels totally soaked in cold water. I broke out on my upper shoulder, and it went down my chest and down my back. Then it turned up on my face and in my ear. I had it for over a year.

I have survived breast cancer. I am cured! I still have leukemia and my white count is always low, but I just have to stay on top of it. I get a blood test every three months, and I have a copy of every blood test. I watch this.

This all drove me to not wait to meet these guys and the girl in the crime. I did not know how long all this was going to wait to kill me, so I had better move. As with my son, something was telling me to move.

I also asked myself, *Is there anything that I haven't seen or done?* My answer was that I did not want to miss one thing that my grandkids were doing. I was driven!

I had heard about restorative justice and victim/offender mediation, but I also had heard that people weren't really doing them. So I started pushing on the system. I was doing lots of talks for the training of Victim Impact for the California Youth Authority, which is why I started talking about why we weren't doing this in jails and the Youth Authority (YA).

I was helping them all with the trainings, so I got a call from someone who was going to do this in the YA. They had to talk to me to get me ready to do this. Talk about open-ended questions versus just yes-and-no answers. We talked for a few hours, and then he went to the only-girls' facility, in Ventura, California, to speak with the girl who took part in my crime. He got her ready too. She agreed to meet with me, and I asked for no table and just chairs set in a circle. She was allowed a counselor and a support person, so there were several people in the room. I found out later a psychologist was there too.

We talked for five and a half hours. I asked her questions about the crime and her part. She still swore that she "just dropped them off." She was not the "getaway driver"! I asked her lots of questions. I told her that I didn't hate her and that I forgave her. She never once said she was sorry. Afterward, I was told that when they debriefed her, she said she told me she was sorry. They all told her that she never said she was sorry. She said, "But I practiced it and practiced it." It has to come from the heart, and it just wasn't there.

I was told that she would get out of YA when she was twenty-five years old. There would be no parole or anyone watching her after she got out. She worked in the YA for TWA (an airline); she made reservations and took people's credit card numbers. A TV show did an exposé on this happening in the CYA, and it all stopped. I asked the superintendent how much money she made while working for TWA. He backed up to the wall and said, "Thousands of dollars." I said, "Gee, I should have sent Roxie to the YA. She could have gotten free counseling and made lots of money." The girl finished high school, got her AA degree, and earned her BA degree, all while she was in the YA. She got out at twenty-five and got her master's degree. She bought a dress shop with the money she earned in the YA.

There was a piece of me that was glad she was doing so well, but there was the mother in me that said, *Really!*

The next one was the guy who had his foot on my back. I couldn't get Corrections moving, so I had a friend with Restorative Justice who was doing work in Solano Prison help me facilitate a victim/offender group. He called and asked me one of the guys' names. "Foot on My Back" was in his group. They had me come up and talk to the group. Of course, they wouldn't let him be in on my talk. I didn't tell the group he was the person involved in my crime. I was able to meet with him behind glass for two hours, and I really pleaded with him to do things right in prison, that I would work to get him out.

While I had cancer, I was in the hospital with a fever from chemo. I got a call from the *Hallmark Channel* asking if they could come film me and, if they could arrange it, have us film a meeting with the guy who had his foot on my back…film in prison. I said, "Good luck with that, but if you can get that done…I'm in!" I did say that I looked like "crap." I didn't have any hair and didn't wear a wig; I wore a scarf and hat.

They called and then came to my house. We filmed me there and then went to Solano Prison. They filmed me meeting him face to face. We talked, and they just filmed. Then we filmed with the victim/offender group. I sat next to him and told the group that he was the person in my crime. They blasted him. I told all of them that I did not want anyone hurting him. Then we sat in a circle with the cameraman in the middle and talked about forgiveness. We were supposed to film for forty minutes or so, but we went on for one and a half hours. It was amazing! *Hallmark* did use our film, but they never used the group film. I felt it was one of the most amazing one and a half hours that I had ever been a part of.

I have been to several board hearings for him. I got the DA to agree to support him getting out and letters from my district attorneys, but when we got to the hearing I found out he had refused to do a urine test. To all of us, it seemed he was using drugs. I told him he would have to be perfect. The board members were not impressed. Trena did go with me as well, and they asked him if he had anything to say. He said that he had apologized to me, but he wanted to apologize to Trena. Trena said that she accepted his apology because he said in the room twice, according to Roxie, not to rape her.

We recently went to a board hearing again. He wanted a cell phone in prison so he could sell drugs; he got caught twice. When they let me talk, I told them not to let him out because he was resorting to his old habits: doing something illegal to get what he wanted.

Before I go any further, I need to tell you what else happened in my life. There is an order to these things:

I continued to work with youth groups at my church, a junior high and a high school youth group. I would go watch my youth group kids play football at Palma High School. The cop on my case, Chuck's son, was playing football too, so I sat with Chuck and Terry Kaiser, the lead investigator on my case. We would meet at all the games and watch together.

Chuck called one of those nights, three and a half years after the murder, and asked how I was doing. He said, "Am I wrong, or are you interested in Terry?" I said, "I can tell he is not interested." I did not know this, but Chuck had called Terry and said, "Hey, stupid, she is interested in you." Terry said, "I do not date victims." Chuck then let me know that he would not date victims.

At the next Friday's football game, he made a comment to me about victims, and I made sure he understood that I AM NOT A VICTIM. I AM A SURVIVOR, so don't ever call a victim.

He would always walk me to the car after the game…for safety. He said as we got to my car, "Maybe we could go have coffee sometime."

I said, "How about now?"

We went to coffee at the Laurel Inn and sat there for hours talking. The funniest thing was, he got out his wallet out and I looked at his whole name: Terry Lee Kaiser. My name is Cheryl Lee Ward; my first husband's name was James Lee Ward. How funny is that! Then I told him my dad was born in Portugal; his was born in Oporto, Portugal. He laughed; his dad had always told him that he should marry a Portuguese girl. Terry had been married for years and had three sons. His first son died from SIDS at three months, and he won custody of his two living sons in his divorce.

The first time I actually met him was at court. He was walking up to the Monterey Courthouse cafeteria. He sat down with the other sheriffs who were going to testify. Chuck was sitting with me, and he said, "That is Sergeant Terry Kaiser; he is also my son's godfather." Chuck mentioned that Terry had quit smoking and had gone back to smoking. So, I got up to go back to court, and I walked behind him and said, "It takes a real man to quit smoking."

He whipped around and said, "Who the h___ is that?"

They all said, "That is Mrs. Ward." That was the first introduction.

We dated for four and a half years before we got married. We had a big wedding. I felt that we all needed to celebrate. People needed to see that we could survive such a big tragedy. Life was not half empty—it was full! My son, Brett, walked me down the aisle. There was a song that I felt the Lord used to give me permission to find my son: "All I Ask of You" from *The Phantom of the Opera*. I walked down the aisle to that song. I asked my son, "Do you remember the significance of this song?" He said, "Yes…and am I glad you found me." I cried all the way down the aisle. It was a day of celebration.

A lot of people asked me why I would marry a cop—the cop who caught them all. Yes, I am enamored with this sheriff. I do not know who I would be if he had not caught them all. I would have driven myself mad looking for them. I know people say it sounds like a movie: I married the guy who caught them all. Nope, not a movie—it's my life!

We went to the board hearing for the guy who was the lookout in the crime at my home. All the way to the California-Mexico border. It was a long trip, and Terry went with me. I went into the hearing and told the lookout I had him cleared too. I spoke for him to get out of prison, and they asked my husband, the sheriff who caught him, what he thought about him getting out. I would never have asked my husband to speak on his behalf. He told the board that he should get out, and the lookout broke down and just bawled. They released him on February 7, 2019. He has done really well. He has a new little son, and he is going back into the prison to give talks about what inmates all need to do to get their act together.

Seven years ago, I was told I could do a victim/offender mediation with the guy who raped Roxie. No one in my family wanted me to do this, and no one would go with me. I drove five and a half hours to Lancaster Prison.

To prepare myself to meet with him, I didn't listen to calming music; no, I told myself over and over, *Shields down…shields down…shields down.* You see, I can be tough, and that is not who had to go into that prison to meet with the guy who raped Roxie. The person who had to go into that prison was Roxie's mom.

When I drove up to the prison, the guy at the gate asked me, "What are you doing here today?" I told him I was going to meet with one of the people involved in my crime.

He said, "What the hell are you doing that for?" Here we go!

I parked a mile away because there was no parking for victims! I walked and walked. I was walking through cars, and then, all of a sudden, I heard a voice: *"Never in your life are you doing more of what I want you to do than right now."* It was God. I have never felt so close or so in step with the Lord. I was overcome with emotion.

I went into the prison, and again they all gave me grief that I was meeting with the person involved in my crime.

We had a person who got us ready to meet, and he had a support person. I already knew the person who got us ready, Suzanne. She worked at California Youth Authority and had me come in during the training of victim/offender mediation. We had become friends. She was the perfect person to get us both ready.

She set down the guidelines, and that was it. I started asking questions, and he said he was going to be completely honest. It took him two hours to look at me. Only when he started asking me about Roxie did he look at me. Then he gave me the apology of a lifetime. He said it was his fault that my husband was murdered. He escalated the crime and caused my husband to die. I was totally surprised at that admission. He told me everything that happened that day, about all the players in the crime. After six hours and one break, they had a siren go off, and we had to end the day. I hugged him when I left. I could tell he was shocked.

A few days later, after I got home, I received a letter from him. His first line said, "You set me free today." I knew that he would feel that way. What I didn't know was that he would set me free. Before I went, I took an envelope with his CDC number on it since I don't have them memorized. When I got home, I went to put it away, and when I looked at the envelope…instead of a flash of him in my bedroom on that day, I saw a flash of the young man who sat across from me in that prison. He is a different young man today. I had been set free too. You can be set free and still be in prison and be free out here and be in prison.

I got a short letter a couple of years ago asking if I would write a letter on his behalf. First, you need to know that he has not one ding against his record in prison. And as other prisoners have told me, that is almost impossible. He has a zero record. You get a ding for stepping on a line. So for thirty years, he kept a perfect record, and that is according to the warden. Now, I wanted to write this letter, but I realized it was not up to me. Roxie had to say it was okay. That would be a miracle.

Roxie…she had a hard time in all of this. She actually was going to kill herself; she had a gun. It took me nine years to be able to say she would survive. Two things made a difference: first a DUI that scared her and then a dog, Kya. The dog was half pit and half Lab. Roxie started working at wineries, and she could take Kya with her to work. I tried to get her to go to counseling, but she resisted. She went to Napa and worked at wineries up there. A boyfriend broke up with her and told her to go to counseling, and she told me months later that she did.

The counselor told her that was enough of the past; let's put together a plan for the future. Roxie told me then she was going to go to Australia to get her wine science degree. Lots of interns came to work in the U.S. from Australia, and they told her to go there to get her degree. It would only take three years there, whereas it would have taken her six here; they don't make you take things that don't apply to your degree. The day she got on the plane, all I could think about was what courage it took for her to do this. No one was going to meet her; she was alone.

She finished college in three years, and she is now a winemaker in a coastal winery. She makes over two million gallons of wine a year. She is not married and has no kids, but she has the greatest, nicest boyfriend in the world. We all just love him.

Every year on the anniversary of Jamie's death, we get together to celebrate his life. This year we went to Santa Cruz; my daughter Trena works there. We went to lunch and to antique shops. Roxie and I came home together alone. She had never asked me about meeting with the guy who raped her. I told her everything he said and how he was doing in prison. I told her that he had asked for me to write a letter on his behalf but that I would only write it if she told me it was okay. I would never mention it again.

Trena got a movie on the way home, *The Shack*. Trena and I had both read the book. We watched the movie, and all cried and then went to bed. Roxie texted me two days later and said, "Write the letter for him to get out. I'm not his judge and jury!"

I couldn't believe it. I immediately wrote him, and he wrote back. He said, "She set me free." He was shocked.

I wrote the letter, but I knew it would take a miracle for him to get a board hearing or to get out. But I know a God who is in charge of miracles.

I still write to all the guys. I write the shooter, but he does not want to meet me using restorative justice. You have to say you are guilty, and he refused to say that. He did say he would put me on his visitor list, but I won't come in that way. It puts lots of people at risk. The system would not like me doing it that way. I believe someday he will agree to meet me, though.

A lot of new laws have come into the system. If you committed a crime under the age of twenty-six but did not commit the murder, you can get the murder charge off your record. The guy who had his foot on my back decided he wanted to get out in this way instead of just keeping himself out of trouble. So last November we went back to court for three days.

Thirty-two people were subpoenaed for this guy. I sat in the hallway for three days before I finally testified. Then the judge said, "You can sit in now."

It was all over. He was denied and still put in an appeal to San Jose Court. He was denied again. Thirty years later, and we were back in court. The lookout, who had already gotten out, put in to have the murder removed off his record but had his attorney say in court that he wanted to remove the petition because he did not want to put us through a trial again. Trena said to tell him thank you.

Thank God for Trena. She could be in court and tell me what was happening. She said she wished she would have been there that night. Roxie and I say that if she would have, we would have probably all been killed because she has a mouth like me. Thank God she was not there. I think she felt left out! Oh, God never would have wanted any more of that on any of us.

CHAPTER 5
16 Years

by Guy

When I told my adoptive parents that I had received free tickets to go to the World Series to watch the Oakland A's play the Los Angeles Dodgers, they were not that surprised. But a year later, when I was unable to contact my birth mother and I was devastated, they were shocked. I became depressed and could not get the problem off my mind. My sisters were concerned, and at one point my father suggested that he would take me to San Francisco and knock on her door.

However, that was not what I wanted. I had told Cheryl in our first meeting that I wanted to be in a room with my birth mother and for the two of us to both be okay with the other one being present. If I had knocked on her door, this would not have happened. For me, the feeling of depression was like having a fear of heights and feeling myself falling, nonstop, for months and years. Getting past this feeling was very burdensome.

It was sixteen years from the time when I first contacted my birth mother until I met her. During this time, I moved four times, bought two houses, and had three jobs. My adoptive mother had died, and one of my sisters had survived a twenty-five-year stint of drug abuse that had started with marijuana and ended with heroin. During this time, she had been in prison, and her husband had died from a drug overdose. My children were twenty and twenty-two, and my daughter had moved to San Diego. I had developed a meaningful relationship with an aunt, an uncle, cousins, a half-brother, and two half-sisters.

When I contacted my mother, it was clear that she was not prepared. In general, nobody in the family knew about me. I made contact with the family through her sister-in-law, a person my birth mother really did not seem to like too much. In addition, although I was aware of the disconnect between these two women, it did not stop me from getting close to my aunt. I was reminded over and over again that my bond with my aunt was a hindrance in my goal of meeting my mother.

When I talked to my uncle, he was interested in business and security. He talked about a lot of things that were interesting, but I wasn't interested so much in the things I could find in a book or from talking to someone else. I wanted to know about him and his roots. I asked him a lot of questions about his family, his mother, his father—who was a twin, where did they come from, have you ever been there? He did not seem to have much interest in this topic, so other than an introduction to the family, where we had out the photo album, we really didn't talk about roots too much.

My aunt was interested in our children, and we heard from her quite often. When we met my half-brother, my son was four. After a nice visit and a long lunch, we had a two-hour drive home. My son announced from the back, "I would like to have a half-brother." I told him that I didn't think that we could arrange that, but he should ask his mother. So, he did. "Mom, can I have a half-brother?" Of course, the answer was no. And with that, he cried the rest of the way home and refused to talk to his mother for three days.

A few months later, my half-brother invited us to join him for a weekend trip to Reno. During this trip, I met one of my half-sisters. She also had a thumb that did not bend, so I was particularly interested in seeing her hands. She had a daughter who was the same age as my daughter. On this first visit, all the kids were pretty quiet while trying to figure out who each other was and what they were like.

A few years later, I met my other half-sister in Alaska. It was the summer equinox. We went out to dinner at about eleven and then talked at the bed-and-breakfast I was staying at until after four in the morning. It was still daylight, so we lost track of time. We took our shoes and socks off to compare feet and toes, as I told her that not only did my thumbs not bend but my feet were slightly different as well.

It took sixteen years from first contact before I was able to meet my mother. The rest of this chapter talks about this journey.

From 1985 to 1995, my adoptive mother was sick. She was first hospitalized with a severe asthma episode and, for the next ten years, was in and out of the hospital on a regular basis with breathing problems. The problems were often life threatening and, over time, became progressively worse. When she was not in the hospital, she was somewhat normal, but as time went on her good days were less good, and she had fewer good days between trips to the hospital.

She and my father had talked about my sister and me finding our roots. As a concept, she had accepted this as something that we might pursue as we got older. Even so, she mentioned in confidence that she feared that our mothers would come back to claim us. My mother's fear was a mountain. My mother was the source of love in my life and in the lives of others. She was the best friend of many of the people who knew her, including some of my friends and friends of my sister. She was able to talk and listen to people and had a way of caring about everyone.

As my mother's health continued to decline, I was overwhelmed with grief and conflicts of interest; my goal of connecting with my birth mother felt like it was taking me away from being present with my adoptive mom. Throughout her life, my mother offered nothing but loving support and understanding to me, and even though she would never want to stop me from finding my birth mother I sensed that watching this part of my journey was hard on her. Adoptees constantly struggle with these feelings of loyalty when family is involved; part of me would always love my mom, and a part of me would always need to find my birth mother. With my mother sick, however, it felt impossible to make peace with that duality; one moment I could be fine and the next, extremely rattled. This instability lasted even after my mother died.

Shortly before Cheryl's husband died, I lost my job in Salinas. I moved back home to Napa to search for work while my wife and kids continued to live in King City. The separation was difficult for me. One weekend I would drive to King City to visit them, and the next they would come to Napa to visit me.

There was a moment in 1991 when it felt like my birth mother was becoming open to meeting me. A cousin had contacted me and told me that she was opening up. In my other family, my mother's health was on a roller-coaster, my sister's drug problems were problematic, my family life was being stressed as I didn't like being away from my wife and children, and I was still out of work. I wrote a letter to my birth mother—bad timing—and it ended all hope of us meeting at that time.

There was another moment, in 1995 or 1996, when it felt like my birth mother would meet me. My half-brother was going to get married, and he wanted me to be at the wedding. For me, this was problematic. My mother had just died, and I was having loyalty issues even though she was no longer present. My sister's drug problems were increasingly worse at that time, and I felt a need to be present in my adoptive family. These feelings were somewhat primal. I could not really put them into words. I wrote my mother a letter, nothing major, "just saying hi," and she was very upset.

A few years after that, I wrote to her and told her, "I want you and I to be on good terms with each other. I want this to be true even if we never meet."

From 1996 to 2006, there were many family gatherings that my birth family had that included my mother. I was simply not invited—although there was talk of "someday, when you meet" that I would hear after each event. There was a desire to know about my birth father, but nobody knew anything about him. My birthmother's husband didn't even know…and I was born just a few months before they were married.

In 1992 I took a job where I traveled all over the country, plus Canada and Mexico. I taught people how to use a phone system that my company manufactured. Later I took a call center job in Sacramento managing the telecom system for a mid-sized to large operation. These two jobs kept my mind away from problems for much of the time—even though I still felt depressed for a lot of this time.

In 2000 I stopped working so hard. Instead of focusing on my problems, I started helping homeless people in my community. At the end of a fourteen-hour day, I was ready to quit my job, and I had decided to do just that. After work, I drove a few blocks to McDonald's and bought a $5 gift certificate. I drove down the street and found a homeless woman sitting on the sidewalk crying. I handed her the certificate. She looked up at me, smiled, and thanked me.

I did not quit the next day.

I had been put on a project where I was supposed to make a process work better. I was told explicitly, "Do not look for money."

Well, that was clear…. The people working on the project did not need my support to do what they wanted to do for the project.

So I looked for money.

I looked through four years of phone bills and vendor bills. I had been a part of the discussion for all of the contracts related to bills that we had paid… but when we paid the bills, they never crossed my desk. As I looked through the mountain of bills, I found all kinds of errors. By the time I was finished, I had recovered over $500,000 for our company. I was given a bonus for my efforts which, over time, was used to help the homeless in the community.

My mission for work with the homeless was to help people that wanted to improve themselves get to a point where they could buy a house. This was a sincere desire, but it was also a message to my sister. Not only could I work through depression without drugs, but I could also help someone who was homeless to buy a house. The message I wanted to create for her was "Don't give up" and "You can do this."

At one point, she reached a low point where someone trying to help her with her recovery told her that ninety-eight percent of the people who get to where she was don't make it out. That was actually a good message for her. She said, "I am the other two percent!" And with that, she put herself on the road to recovery.

My cousin in my birth family had three children, two boys and a girl. When it was time, the oldest, one of the boys, had his bar mitzvah. This was a big event. My aunt and my cousin decided that they wanted me to be there with my wife and children. My birth mother was invited as well. This was an event that was probably a year in the making, so there were many details. The details of getting my birth mother and me both to the event were probably the most complicated.

I didn't say so, but my first reaction when I heard about this was "I don't want to go." I had just about given up hope of meeting her, and sixteen years later I was concerned about what could go wrong. I worried about ruining the day. This was in the summer of 2006.

July 29, 2006, was the big day. My wife and kids, who were twenty-two and twenty, were with me. My daughter had flown up from San Diego to be able to join us for the event. As we pulled into the driveway and parked, there was a car in front of us that entered the parking lot from another entrance. An older man and woman were in that car. We get out of our car, they got out of their car, and we walked together into the synagogue.

It was the first time any of us had been to a Jewish service of any kind. We enjoyed the event and felt welcomed. Afterward, there was lunch. Of course, the couple from the parking lot were right in front of us. My half-sisters came and talked to me. One of them got the attention of the woman in front of me in line and then introduced us.

She told the woman, "This is Guy," and me, "This is our mother."

And with that, we shook hands, smiled at each other, got our food, and went to separate tables.

To honor her wish of not bothering her with questions, I went to a table that was not very close to her table. We all enjoyed lunch, and then my daughter asked her if it was okay for us to get together for pictures. My daughter is the one who convinces the cat to take a bath. She can convince you of anything. So before we knew it, we had gathered for a few pictures: one picture with my birth mother and children and another with my two half-sisters. It was amazing how similar our facial features were.

Now, during these sixteen years, it would have been easy to ask, "Where is God in all of this?"

I remember the day that I met Cheryl. I showed her a prayer card. It had a picture of Jesus at the beach and "Footprints in the Sand."[2] In the story, there was a place where there was only one set of footprints.

"Where was Jesus?"

"It was at this time that I was carrying you."

I remember wanting to be present in a room with my birth mother and for neither of us to have a problem with the presence of the other person.

I also remember Cheryl wanting to be present if there was a time when her son got married. Well, guess what. He was married that same weekend.

At that moment, I stopped feeling that I had failed all of this time and started feeling that God wanted me to travel down a different path.

In addition to meeting my goal and Cheryl meeting her goal, there were people who had been homeless in Vacaville who had eventually purchased homes. I didn't do much of the work, but I did plant the seeds.

My sister also got off of drugs, went back to work, and got married.

My adoptive mother died in 1995. I wish she could have seen my story come to this conclusion.

It ain't over yet.

$$\text{CHAPTER 6}$$
Getting Past Roadblocks

by Guy

From 2006 to 2012, there were six other events both I and my birth mother attended. Each event was a little different. In each event, there was that awkward moment where I walked up to my birth mother, said hello, and told her that I hoped she was having a good time. In general, I did not push her beyond this. She would smile and thank me for being there…and then move on to another conversation. My half-sisters had talked to her and encouraged her to be more engaged, but she just could not.

They also asked questions about my father. It seemed like some of what she told them was true and some maybe not so much. I don't know if she forgot or if she wanted to keep them from finding him.

In any event, the piece of the puzzle that included my birth father was always a bit of a blur.

When I had searched for my birth mother, it seemed that she and I had been connected. I searched for her at three colleges she had attended. I felt odd when I traveled to one area in San Francisco. It was near where she had grown up. There were a lot of things that were like this that made me feel that we had a link even though we never talked to each other.

My birth father was a different story. I was almost certain that he had died at around the time of my birth. I felt that he had jumped from the Golden Gate Bridge and drowned. I had this dream over and over for many years. I had even pinpointed the date that this happened: June 30.

In August 2012 there was another family event. My niece was getting married. This was my birth mother's granddaughter—someone she had been in contact with a great deal and had a very strong relationship with. When I said hello to my birth mother at this event, it was different. When she said hello back to me, she was glowing. She was very excited, and it was clear that she could not have been happier.

It was clear to me that my birth mother might be receptive to having a personal conversation with me. I sent a voicemail message to my half-sister, informing her of my thoughts. She did not get my message, but she did tell me that my birth mother wanted to meet with me and had invited me to see her.

During 2012 my birth mother's health was declining. I did not get all the details, but I thought I understood that she may have had a heart attack and a stroke. In any event, she was in declining health. When I met with her, she was in the hospital. I talked to her with my sister for a few minutes, and then I left.

My birth mother was moved to a nursing home in Sacramento, and for over two weeks the only person available to visit her was me. Additionally, she wanted to meet me.

Her nursing home may have had forty or fifty beds. When I would visit, there was maybe one other person there who had a visitor, so all of the other people who were staying there would look at me, wanting to be the one with a visitor. During a two-week period of time, I was able to visit her five times. As a second career, I had become a high school math teacher. I spent my time telling her stories of students in my class. Most of the stories were pretty funny. She would almost always tell me, "That was an interesting story." On the second week, on Friday, it was my fifth visit. I was there for about two hours, which was a little longer than most of my visits.

After I had told her my stories, she told me that she wanted to see my wife when I came again. And before I left, she said, "I have a funny story to tell you."

Then she stared into space. She looked at the wall for maybe thirty seconds. Then she said, "But it wasn't funny to me."

Then she stared into space, not telling her story.

It was reported that she died that night, but in looking back it felt like she may have died trying to tell me her story. It seemed to me that she died trying to tell me the story about my father.

A lot of people would think that this was a tragic ending. The event in 2006, where we met for the first time, was my goal with my birth mother. I got more than I expected by being able to talk to her one on one at a time when I was the only person available to see her. I considered this time to be a blessing.

But like I said in the last chapter, "It ain't over yet."

My half-brother told me that his father had given him the name of my father. He also gave me a picture of a bunch of young people, possibly at a prom. It had a picture of my birth mother with a young man.

From time to time, I would hear from my half-sisters. Similarly, they were interested in knowing more about my birth father. I tracked down a man with the name that fit the description that I had of my birth father. I later talked to him and found out that he was not the one I was looking for. I thought to myself, *Of course not. My birth father is dead.*

I let this go.

Then, a few years later, I noticed that I had a DNA match with a woman not linked to my mother's side of the family. I was able to find out that this was indeed my half-sister.

I contacted her. She did not want to meet me, but I was able to get information about my birth father. He did not die when I was young. He died in 2017. With the half-sister on my father's side, I shared the stories that my birth mother found interesting. When it was clear that she was not interested in meeting me, I had her give me information about my father in exchange for no more contact with her.

CHAPTER 7
Reflections

by Guy

Looking back at our adoption stories, it is clear to me that the support of my wife and children was very important to me. When I needed to correct my course, they would help me understand that I was on the wrong path.

My adoptive family supported me as well. There were never angry words about my search or about the people in my birth family, only concern.

My relationship with each of my three cousins in my birth family was very important. My aunt and uncle helped also, as they made me feel safe and kept somewhat of an emotional firewall between me and my birth mother.

Support from a few close friends was also very important, as I had a place to go when I needed to vent frustrations.

My relationship with Cheryl and her adoption, crime, and cancer stories provided me several important things to look at. Cheryl forgave her father and later forgave the people who entered her home. She said that she did this to free up emotions inside of her; it was not to help the other people. When I heard this, I understood that one of my problems that kept me from meeting my birth mother was that I had never forgiven her. By the time my birth mother and I met, I had. And when we were talking six years after that, there was no anger left inside of me.

During one of my last visits to the nursing home, a nurse asked me if this was my mother. I nodded. Then she asked my mother if she enjoyed the visit from her son. She said, "We are not related. We are just really good friends." Even at that late date, she had a need to hide something.

At her funeral, I was announced by the rabbi as her son. There were many people, more than a dozen, who were whispering, trying to figure this out. Afterward, when we had lunch, I was introduced to everyone. Most of these people were related to my birth mother's husband.

In the aftermath of the crime story, Cheryl had told me that if the people who entered her house had just asked her husband for a job at his worksite, he would have given it to them since the primary reason for the crime was to acquire money. What this did for me is cause me to be proactive in my help of people in need. I went out and gave gift certificates to McDonald's to people who were homeless. I worked with people in shelters to improve their situations. I did what I could to remove reasons that people had that might cause them to commit a crime. In one case, someone specifically told me that my advice and support had stopped him from committing a crime.

When I look at Cheryl's story, the crime in her house happened the very night she had been to the support group, Search Finders, to talk about what it was like to meet her son. She was as happy as she could be at that time. She later told me that had I not "given her permission" to find her son, she would not have looked for him at that time, and she thinks the other things related to the crime would have probably kept her from searching later. Having her son in her life at this very dark time was a light in a dark canyon. It was the thing that brought her balance and happiness when all that she was dealing with was painful and bitter.

There are many places in these two stories to see where the lack of a good father figure was an issue. My birth father was unable to marry my mother. Cheryl's father had abused her. Her husband had fathered a child they did not keep. The people who entered the home did not have good relations with their fathers. The point of this is that I have addressed people at church support groups or in men's groups where husbands or fathers have had issues to resolve.

One of the things that I often said while I was slowly but methodically building support for the homeless program in my community was that I was trying to "change the course of the tide with the force of a feather."

What this meant was that I had a huge task, and I tried to fix it very slowly but consistently.

When I look back at the twenty-two years with my birth mother, this was also in play. When I found success, it was because I worked very slowly and never pushed hard.

When I found my half-sister on my father's side, the timing was bad. It was just before things were happening with the pandemic, and there was a long time between contacts at first because other things were going on. When I did contact her after that, I sent a few letters, telling a few stories, then eventually stopped. I agreed to stop contacting her in exchange for basic information about my birth father.

It was an amazing relief to discover that he had not died in the 1960s. I had dreams for years that he had jumped from the Golden Gate Bridge and died. I was happy to *finally* find out that this was not the case.

In the 1950s and early 1960s, it was common for women who were pregnant with children that they could not raise to place their baby for adoption. This was most often done through a closed adoption.

Two things came out of my first conversation with Cheryl. Birth mothers do not forget, and neither do adoptees forget. An irrational request from some adoptees is that their voice should be part of the decision. Should I have been placed for adoption? I can only answer for me. I would have had a reduced burden had I been placed in an open adoption. Thinking about "the grass is always greener on the other side," I am aware that this may have caused other problems that I could never go back and relive and evaluate.

Faith was a big part of my story. It was never more present than when Cheryl was at her son's wedding on the same weekend that I met my birth mother for the first time.

I started this book by saying that those who enter our journey feel like we have entered our own personal storm that never ends when we find difficulty.

A quote on the bottom of Cheryl's most recent email to me said: "Life isn't about waiting for the storm to pass. It's about learning how to dance in the rain." Cheryl said that she is a survivor. It seems to me that maybe she is more than that. She is an adventurer.

Back in 1983, we had some of the most intense rain that I had ever seen. I was twenty-one. I took my thirteen-year-old cousin with me, and we went rafting on a lake, more like a stream, that was generally very calm. On this day, there were whitecaps throughout the water. It was raining hard, and the wind was blowing. Additionally, my cousin was concerned because the raft had a hole in it, and the boat was starting to take on water. Instinctively, he started trying to get the water out. He was terrified. I told him to stop and gave him one of the oars, and we rowed to the side. He was very scared, and to this day he reminds me of this trip. Alternatively, I was very excited about being there and having the opportunity to make it out—pure adventure.

There was a significant thing that happened when Cheryl and I talked for the first time that was repeated when we went to the support group. Having adoptees, birth parents, and adopted parents talk to each other, when they never had before, was a healing process for most of the people involved.

When Cheryl was later trying to find information about why her family was chosen for the crime, the only people that she could talk to were the people who were involved in the crime. Cheryl pushed for the opportunity to talk to them.

Additionally, I was told that a program was developed for schools to pair bullies with the people they bullied and allow them to tell each other their stories, hopefully causing a reduced opportunity for this to repeat.

Cheryl mentions having a question from God: *"Do you trust me?"*

My friend Dan had a dream at the beginning of 1980, the year he had his heart transplant. In that dream, Jesus told him, *"Trust me."* This feeling of trust was a powerful part of both of these stories. It seems so fitting.

CHAPTER 8
Reflections

by Cheryl

Wow, the people whom God has put in my life.

As I reflect back on how I have managed to survive all this "crap," the only answer is my faith. When I look at the abuse as a child, I thank God for it. It taught me to be a survivor. I looked at the *why* behind my dad's violence toward me; I looked at the fact that he wouldn't take phone calls, how he would come home from work and be so angry. It wasn't about me; it was about him. He was a very short, maybe five feet, four inches, and from Portugal. He had to quit school in fifth grade because his dad died—the dad who beat him even though his dad only had one leg. He'd had his leg cut off because he had a sore that didn't heal. My dad was the only boy, so he had to go to work to support the family. He had three sisters and his mother to take care of and grew up to be an angry man. I realized that since he couldn't fight back against the world, I became his way of letting out his anger.

The abuse taught me to survive. The last time my dad hit me was when I was seventeen years old. I was next door visiting my neighbor, and he felt I should be home. When I came in, he hit me. I looked him straight in the eye and asked him, "Do you feel better now?"

I had figured it all out. It didn't have anything to do with me; it was about him. He hated being short. His dad died when he was in fifth grade. He was the only boy with three sisters, and he had to go to work to support them. He was always angry. His dad used to kick him even though he only had one leg. All my dad knew was hard work and alcohol. He needed

53

someone to take all his anger out on, and it was me. It wasn't my older sister, who would cry before he even hit her; she did everything right. I did everything wrong. When he hit me at seventeen, I didn't cry. He couldn't make me cry. I had gotten tough. I wanted out.

I got tougher and tougher! Hard would be the word. You stop really trusting people that tell you they love you. If your mother and dad don't love you, why should anyone else? When I came back from Holy Family Adoption Agency and Jamie wanted to marry me, I felt so grateful! How could anyone love me? I was lower than low! I gave up my child. I felt so worthless.

When I was young, I went to Catholic school. I am sure that God is the only thing that helped me survive. I used to go to silent retreats. (Anyone who knows me can't believe I can be silent for three days.) I loved those retreats. They would always keep me on track. It took a day and a half for my head to shut up so I could start to listen to the small whisper of the Lord.

I married Jamie at St. Mary's Catholic Church. I had Trena right away after we got married. Then I tried for seven years to get pregnant again. I had two miscarriages. Don't let anyone tell you that it is nothing or no big deal! It was a big deal. I wanted another child so badly. I used to say, "What good could ever come from this?" How many times when I worked at the crisis pregnancy center did girls come in pregnant and then have a miscarriage? God used those miscarriages so many times. I never told anyone that it was "no big deal."

Talk about taking the fun out of marriage—just work at trying to get pregnant! My husband was still gone six months out of every year, and that didn't make it any better. When I got pregnant with Roxie, I didn't tell anyone I was pregnant for four months. I was so afraid of losing another baby. I couldn't listen to anyone's "advice" anymore, so I kept it a secret even from my husband.

I was so thrilled. We were all so thrilled. My daughter Trena was thrilled she was having a baby sister or brother; she felt it was hers too. She was the first person I called with the news. Thank God for small schools that let kids come to the phone with news like that. She screamed in delight! Of course, Jamie was in Oxnard and couldn't make it home. When my water broke, I drove myself to the hospital and had Roxie two hours later. They were almost eight years apart, so they will always be in different stages of their lives.

God had a plan for my life, and I was beginning to see the underside of the plan. I had started going to church every day for Mass. I was moving closer and closer to the Lord.

I started helping people find the Lord in their lives. Then the light turned on for me regarding the Lord. I realized that God would never punish me regarding getting pregnant. Instead, I began to understand that God would use that part of my life…but for what? Then I went to work at the crisis pregnancy center, and all of a sudden all the moments of my life were being used for good—the abuse, the crisis pregnancy, and the miscarriages. God had a plan, and the plan was a perfect plan. *"Do you trust me?"* has become a mantra in my life! I had someone who did love me unconditionally: the Lord. No matter what…He loved me!

When I decided to find Brett, I needed to tell my kids about him. I was so scared. Trena was really shocked, and Roxie was delighted; she said she always wanted a brother. They couldn't wait to meet him. A few months after their dad died, Brett flew into San Jose Airport, and we picked him up.

They started comparing their feet and their toes. It was so funny. What joy he brought to our lives in the middle of the biggest terror we were experiencing. God's grace poured out on us all.

Would I have looked for him after the crime? I wonder! Thank God I had him in our lives after the murder—a light in the darkness.

I could never have survived any of this without God.

This year my husband Terry died of pneumonia. I couldn't see him for eight days because they knew it was COVID. God knows how many tests and biopsies were done on his lungs. I had to tell him he was dying. He had damage done to his lungs taking down meth labs while working the drug detail. He had three labs blow up on him. When I told him he was dying, he said, "All I want is to see my grandkids before I die." So, for four days we marched in all the grandkids we could get in to see him. He said his goodbyes to each of them. I stayed 24/7 for four days. I asked him what he wanted for his funeral. He said he wanted the priest who married us to do the funeral, and he wanted to have the service at my church. It was so hard, but he was still sitting up and talking when Roxie and Rachelle, our granddaughter, were the last ones to come in.

I told the doctors and nurses to make him comfortable. Early Sunday morning, September 26, I got a message from my friend Faye. She said, "Say the 'Our Father' in his ear, Cheryl." I went over and prayed the "Our Father" in his ear, and I watched him breathe his last breath.

We had the funeral at St. Joseph's Church and the reception at our home, the same house that I lived in before. The house that my husband died in…. Yes, I still live in that house. I still sleep in that bedroom. The flashbacks are not in the house; they are in my mind. I did not run from what happened to me. We built this house; it was my plan. Then, when I married Terry, he made a "park" out of the backyard. We have almost six acres. Terry created an amazingly beautiful place. He was a Baptist, and he gave me the Stations of the Cross for a Christmas present. He made a pathway lined with roses for the Station journey. We have lots of rose bushes. They all have to smell; I think it is a sin if they don't smell. We had his reception in his beautiful creation. His friends got up and talked about him, and his grandkids got up and shared all the funny stories about dealing with him. Trena got up and talked about what Terry brought to this family; we all needed to feel safe, and he brought that to this family. I remember on our first date at the air show in Salinas, he reached back and grabbed my hand. I knew then that I was safe. He knew I felt that too.

I know Jamie and Terry are up in heaven talking about me. I have to find things to laugh about in God's plan for my life.

Two months after the funeral for Terry, my son Brett's stepdaughter, Brittnee, got married in our backyard. Terry wanted them to go ahead with the wedding, and it meant the world to us that they would have it at our home. Terry was honored that she wanted to get married here. It couldn't have been more perfect. Two hundred-plus people and the weather was great. Everyone was told it would be cold, so when the sun went down out came the fur coats. Everyone had gone to antique stores and bought old fur coats. It was all so cool.

Trena just moved to Nashville, and her youngest, Shanon, is already there. Rachelle will leave in May. We went for Christmas, so I didn't sit around being sad. It was great. I love to dance, and we danced for three nights. You don't have to have anyone to dance with, so I just danced alone. I did get asked to dance at a couple of places. I laughed because my daughter and granddaughters, who are all so cute, were not asked to dance…just me.

No, I'm not moving to Nashville. I will go visit, but I am going to stay in this beautiful place that we built. Of course, I have to mow the four acres of grass. I can hear Terry laughing about that. It takes me four to five hours to mow. I'm seventy-seven but I still run, and I dance.

I read a card that I have put up on the refrigerator: "Life isn't about waiting for the storm to pass; it's about learning to dance in the rain."

That is my new motto.

I have to know that God has a plan, and it is the perfect plan. There is no such thing as an accidental life or an accidental death. God is in both. It doesn't happen without Him. So, my next chapter is ahead of me…. I am waiting.

Footnotes

[1] Search Finders is a search and support group for adoptees, birthparents and significant others. Dot was a lady that helped people make connections. The organization was in San Jose from 1973 to sometime after 2000. It is no longer operating.

[2] Footprint in the Sand
Authorship is disputed.

It is likely to have been written by Margaret Powers, Carolyn Carty or Mary Stevenson. It may have been written in 1964.

In Guy's story, he held this prayer card and read it to Cheryl during their first visit. He told her that it would be nice to feel God's presence now. After the reunion with his birth mother in 2006 and Cheryl's attendance at her son's wedding, the message on the card was confirmed.